Dad
Tell Me Your Story

Keepsake Journal

Hannah Maiwald

ISBN: 979-8-4160-8735-7

1st edition

represented by

Philipp Eyl
Anni-Eisler-Lehmann-Strasse 8a
55122 Mainz
GERMANY

Hi!

My name is Hannah Maiwald and I'm an independent aut-hor from Germany. I would like to thank you so much for choosing my „Dad Tell Me Your Story" Keepsake Journal. Every time I start a new project, I think about how I can make my book as engaging and inspiring as possible. My „Tell Me Your Story" Series of Keepsake Journals for Mom, Dad, Grandma and Grandpa has been a particularly heartfelt project that I have invested a lot of time and energy into. I hope you can tell that from this book. If you like, you can share your thoughts about this book with other people, for example in the form of a review on Amazon. By writing a review on Amazon, you can give other customers a better idea of why the book is hopefully worth buying. In any case, I hope that with this book I have been able to contribute to bringing you and your father even closer together than you hopefully already are.

Sincerely

Hannah

CHAPTERS

1

Profile

Please paste a recent picture of yourself.

Profile

What is your full name?

When and where were you born?

How tall and heavy were you at birth?

Do you have any distinguishing marks?

2

Birth and Preschool

Please paste a picture of you as a baby, in kindergarten or in other situations from your early years.

Birth and Preschool

Are there any stories you have been told about your birth? What do you know about your first days on planet Earth?

What special or cute stories did your parents tell you about yourself as a baby?

Birth and Preschool

What is your earliest memory?

Who were your most important caregivers in the first three years?

Were you named after someone and if so, who? Do you like your name or would you rather have it changed?

Birth and Preschool

Did you have a favorite stuffed animal when you were little? If so, can you still describe it?

What do you know or remember about the house you lived in when you were a baby? How long did you live there?

Did you go to kindergarten? If so, what did you like best there?

Birth and Preschool

Here is some additional space for other baby stories or preschool memories you'd like to share with me.

3
Childhood

Please paste a childhood photo of your-self, e.g. from your first day at school, from vacation with your parents, ...

Childhood

How and where did you usually spend your free time when you were little?

What were your favorite activities and hobbies? What kind of games did you like to play with your friends?

Childhood

When did you start school? Can you still remember your first day at school?

Did you have a nickname? If so, who gave it to you and why?

Did you receive any pocket money? If so, how much was it and what did you spend it on?

Childhood

What was your favorite food as a child? Who cooked it for you?

What was your favorite movie or show that you watched as a child?

What nostalgic tastes, sounds or smells instantly take you back to your childhood?

Childhood

Did you have pets? If so, tell me about them. What pets did you have? What were their names?

Do you remember any fears from your childhood? What were you most afraid of as a child?

Childhood

Were there any rituals at meals or at bedtime? Are there certain books or songs that your parents read or sang to you?

Is there anything you miss about being a kid?

Childhood

Did you ever break your arms or legs as a child? If so, how did that happen?

If you compare your childhood with today's situation: What did you have as a child that a child probably doesn't have today?

What would you say? Did you grow up in an affluent household, in the middle class, or in a low-income household?

Childhood

Did you like the town or village where you grew up? Why yes, why not?

What is your fondest childhood memory?

Childhood

Would you say that you had a happy childhood? Why yes, why not?

Childhood

Here is some additional space for notes and other childhood memories you'd like to share with me.

4

Your Parents

Please paste a picture from your mom here.

Your Parents

Where is your mother from?

Describe your mother in no more than three sentences.

What qualities or skills did you inherit from your mother?

What is your favorite memory about your mom?

Please paste a picture from your dad here.

Your Parents

Where is your father from?

Describe your father in no more than three sentences.

What qualities or skills did you inherit from your father?

What is your favorite memory about your dad?

Your Parents

What did your parents do for a living? What was their profession?

Do you know how and when your parents met?

Your Parents

What is the best advice your mother gave you?

What is the best advice your father gave you?

Your Parents

What do you admire or appreciate the most about your parents?

What traditions of your parents did you pass on to me?

Your Parents

Here is some additional space for notes and other memories about your parents that you'd like to share with me.

5

Family

Please paste a picture of you and your family, e.g. at family reunions, birthday parties, or other special events.

Family

Have you ever met your great-grandparents? If so, what do you remember about them?

How did you get along with your siblings? If you don‘t have a brother or sister: Did you ever wish you had siblings?

Family

How was your relationship with your grandparents? Did you ever meet them? Did you enjoy being with them and what did you do with them?

Family

What did your grandmother have in common with your mother?

What did your grandfather have in common with your father?

Family

Do you take after your mother or father? What do you base that on?

Did you have a stronger bond with your mother or father? Why?

Family

What things do you not know about your parents that you would really like to know?

Were there any other adult role models in your childhood? Who were they and what made them important to you?

Family

Have there ever been difficulties or major disputes in your family that had to be overcome? What caused them and were they ever resolved?

Family

Did your family have regular gatherings or celebrations when you were growing up? What special events did your family celebrate each year?

Family

Here is some additional space for notes and other family memories you'd like to share with me.

6

Teenager

Please paste a picture from you as a teenager, e.g. together with your highschool friends.

Teenager

How would you describe yourself as a teenager?

How did your relationship with your parents change during adolesence?

Teenager

Did you have a close circle of friends back then? If so, do you still have contact with your friends?

Who was your "homie" during your teenage years? Do you still have contact with him?

Teenager

Have you ever been rebellious as a teenager? How did you test boundaries? Did you ever have punk phases?

How were you disciplined when you did something that upset your parents? How did you react when you had trouble with your parents?

Teenager

Were your parents strict? Did you have to be home at a certain time?

Did you have braces? How long and how did you feel about it?

Have you ever had a crush on someone famous? If so, who was it?

Teenager

Have you ever gone on vacation with your family? If so, tell me about some of the memories you have from those vacations.

Teenager

In retrospect, what do you wish you had known earlier as a teenager?

What is your fondest memory of your youth?

Teenager

Here is some additional space for notes and other memories from your youth that you'd like to share with me.

7

School

Please paste a picture from your high school years, e.g. pictures from enrollment or your graduation.

School

Let‘s be honest: Did you like going to school or not so much? :-)

Did you sometimes skip school? If so, what did you do during that time?

School

Did you tend to have good or bad grades? Did you ever have to stay down a year?

What were your favorite subjects and what were your hated subjects?

What subject that is not taught do you think should definitely be taught in school?

School

Did you have a favorite teacher and if so, what was his or her name? Why was he or she your favorite teacher?

Did you participate in any extracurricular activities? For example, were you in a sports club at school or did you play an instrument?

School

Do you have any special memories from your high school days? Tell me about them.

School

Here is some additional space for notes and other memories from school you‘d like to share with me.

8

Let‘s talk about your „Firsts“!

Let‘s talk about your „Firsts“!

What brand and model was your first car? When did you get it?

____

How old were you when you had your first kiss?

____

When did you go on your first date?

____

When did you buy or get your first mobile phone?

____

At what age did you leave home and move into your first own apartment?

____

When did you have your first boyfriend? What was his name?

____

When did you attend your first concert?

____

Let‘s talk about your „Firsts“!

What was the first record (CD, tape, ...) you bought?

What was your first pet? When did you get it?

What was your first job? How much did you get paid?

At what age did you drink alcohol for the first time?

Where did you go on your first vacation without your parents?

Who was the first non-family member you cooked a meal for?

What was the first foreign country you travelled to?

9

Let‘s talk about your „Favorites“!

Let‘s talk about your „Favorites“!

What is your favorite food?

What is your favorite drink?

What is your favorite fruit?

What is your favorite dessert?

What is your favorite candy?

What is your favorite spice?

What is your favorite flower?

Let‘s talk about your „Favorites“!

What is your favorite car?

What is your favorite animal?

What is your favorite color?

What is your favorite quote?

What is your favorite language?

What is your favorite book?

What is your favorite music genre?

Let‘s talk about your „Favorites“!

What is your favorite city?

___

What is your favorite country?

___

What is your favorite fashion brand?

___

What is your favorite season?

___

What is your favorite flower?

___

What is your favorite smell?

___

What is your favorite holiday or annual celebration?

___

Let‘s talk about your „Favorites“!

What is your favorite way to spend a sunday?

What is your favorite way to relax after a busy day?

What is your favorite sports team?

Who is your favorite actor?

Who is your favorite actress?

Who is your favorite comedian?

Who is your favorite singer?

10

Dad‘s Trivia

Dad‘s Trivia

Do you have a guilty pleasure? What is it?

What kind of behavior always makes you angry?

What do you think is the best decision you have ever made?

Dad's Trivia

Tell me something about yourself that you think most people, including me, probably don't know.

Have you ever been in a life-threatening situation? How did you get into it and how did you get out of it?

Dad's Trivia

What is the one thing you've always wanted to overcome?

What is the most expensive thing you have ever bought for yourself?

What is the greatest gift you have ever received? What was it and who did you get the gift from?

Dad's Trivia

When you look back, what do you wish you had wasted less time on? Why?

What has been your favorite decade or period in your life so far? Why?

11

Personal Values and Beliefs

Personal Values and Beliefs

Do you believe in life after death?

What influence did your parents' faith have on your life? Were you raised religiously?

Was there ever a time in your life when you went to church regularly? Why yes, why not?

Personal Values and Beliefs

Do you support any charities? If so, why are these charities important to you?

How have your spiritual or religious beliefs changed over the course of your life?

Personal Values and Beliefs

Would you consider yourself a patriot? Why yes, why not?

Have you ever been to a demonstration? Against what? If not, why not?

Have you ever thought about getting into politics yourself? Why yes, why not?

Personal Values and Beliefs

How have your political views or personal values changed over the years? What were you convinced of in the past that you now see very differently?

What do you think about the political views of your children's generation?

Personal Values and Beliefs

Is there a politician who has particularly impressed or influenced you? If so, in what way?

What three things would you change if you had the power to do so?

Personal Values and Beliefs

Has anything socially or politically significant happened in your life that you hope future generations will be spared?

During your lifetime, technology has developed enormously. Does life seem simpler or more complicated to you today?

12

Becoming a Father

Please paste a picture of you when you played with me or held me as a baby.

Becoming a Father

Tell me about the moment you realized you were becoming a father for the first time.

How did the mother tell you the „big news“?

Becoming a Father

What was your biggest concern before the birth of your first child?

How did you feel and what went through your mind when you held me in your arms for the first time?

Becoming a Father

How did you put your children to bed? Was it hard to get me to sleep? Did I cry a lot?

At what age could I walk? Do you remember what my first words were? How old was I?

Do you remember the first birthday present you bought for me? What was it?

Becoming a Father

In what ways did your expectation of being a dad differ from your experience of being a dad?

In what ways has your life changed the most after becoming a father for the first time?

Becoming a Father

What advice would you like to give to young fathers today?

What do you think can be called "the perks of being a father"?

Becoming a Father

Here is some additional space for notes and other memories or advice about fatherhood and raising children you'd like to share with me.

13

Romance and Relationships

Romance and Relationships

Do you believe in love at first sight? Have you ever experienced it yourself?

What is your fondest memory of your first great love?

Romance and Relationships

How did your parents shape your attitude toward relationships?

Have you ever had a girlfriend that your parents didn't like, and how did you handle that situation?

Romance and Relationships

What do you think is the secret of a long and happy relationship?

What mistake should men never make in a relationship?

Romance and Relationships

How and when did you meet my mother? What did you like most about her?

Romance and Relationships

Here is some additional space for notes and other thoughts about love and relationships that you'd like to share with me.

14
Work and Career

Work and Career

How did you choose your profession? Who or what particularly influenced you in your choice of profession?

What career decisions would you make differently today if you had the chance?

Work and Career

What is your definition of success?

Have you ever had major financial problems? If so, how did they arise and how did you overcome them?

Work and Career

What was your dream job as a child and what job did your parents want for you?

What was the best job you ever had? Why this one in particular?

Which job did you dislike the most? Why?

Work and Career

Where did you first live after you moved out of your parents' home? Did you live there alone or with others?

Which of the places or cities you have lived in do you have the best memories of?

What things do you consider to be a total waste of money? Why?

Work and Career

What was one of the most stressful periods in your career and how did you deal with it?

What books have most influenced your thinking, your work, or your life, and in what ways have they affected you?

Work and Career

Do you have any other thoughts about schools or education in general that you think would be helpful or important to know?

15

Notes to those I love

Notes to those I love

If there is anything else you would like to say or tell me, then here is some space to let me know.